Picnics &
Hampers

Notes

1. Standard level spoon measurements are used in all recipes.
1 tablespoon = one 15 ml spoon
1 teaspoon = one 5 ml spoon

2. Both imperial and metric measurements have been given in all recipes. Use one set of measurements only and not a mixture of both.

3. Eggs should be medium unless otherwise stated. The Department of Health advises that eggs should not be consumed raw. This book contains dishes made with raw or lightly cooked eggs. It is prudent for more vulnerable people such as pregnant and nursing mothers, invalids, the elderly, babies and young children to avoid uncooked or lightly cooked dishes made with eggs. Once prepared, these dishes should be kept refrigerated and used promptly.

4. Milk should be full fat unless otherwise stated.

5. Fresh herbs should be used unless otherwise stated. If unavailable, use dried herbs as an alternative but halve the quantities stated.

6. Ovens should be pre-heated to the specified temperature – if using a fan-assisted oven, follow manufacturer's instructions for adjusting the time and the temperature.

7. Pepper should be freshly ground black pepper unless otherwise stated.

8. Nuts and nut derivatives.
This book includes dishes made with nuts and nut derivatives. It is advisable for readers with known allergic reactions to nuts and nut derivatives and those who may be potentially vulnerable to these allergies, such as pregnant and nursing mothers, invalids, the elderly, babies and children, to avoid dishes made with nuts and nut oils. It is also prudent to check the labels of pre-prepared ingredients for the possible inclusion of nut derivatives.

9. Vegetarians should look for the 'V' symbol on a cheese to ensure it is made with vegetarian rennet. There are vegetarian forms of Parmesan, Feta, Cheddar, Cheshire, Red Leicester, dolcelatte and many goats' cheeses, among others.

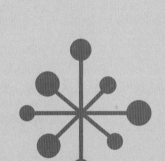

Picnics & Hampers

text Marie Abadie

photographs Jean-Pierre Dieterlen

design Marianne Paquin

HACHETTE
Illustrated

preface

Going on a picnic is like embarking on an adventure trip with your dining room tucked firmly under your arm. At the end of the trail a corner of nature awaits you. Look, how about there? On that shady bank by the stream? Like an invading army, you quickly stake your claim, spread your cloth on an imaginary table and set it with real food. A picnic means leaving table manners locked in the cupboard – to the delight of the child inside us all! It means dispensing with cutlery and eating with your fingers, shedding inhibitions, forgetting about diets and just enjoying it all.

Picnicking is a part of being on holiday. So, here I have filled my baskets with produce from everywhere, as each season offers its bounty.

Lunch on the grass in June, on boat trips or in a shady wood; a menu to please weekend painters, or lovers; cherries playfully worn as earrings and cherries baked in a clafoutis. In summer, tortillas, gambas with pimientos and sangria are in perfect harmony with the waves on an Atlantic beach. Sheltering from the wind in a grey-blue rocky inlet? That's just the right moment to open up the hamper and bring out an olive and thyme bread, still warm from the oven. On the coastal road beside the Channel, the smell of a citrus-flavoured cake will mingle temptingly with the mist.

Marie Abadie

fishing trips
and lakesides

Festive tomatoes
with tartare, guacamole and cottage cheese fillings

Preparation time.
30 min

Serves 6

**1 kg (2 lb) cherry
vine tomatoes**

1 avocado

**125 g (4 oz)
mayonnaise**

**125 g (4 oz)
cottage cheese**

**$\frac{1}{2}$ teaspoon grated
lemon rind**

**4 tablespoons
lemon juice**

**2 tablespoons
capers**

$\frac{1}{2}$ bunch of chervil

1 mint sprig

Tabasco

**3 tablespoons
olive oil**

salt, pepper

1. Remove the tomatoes from the vine, leaving just the flower stalk attached, and put in an airtight container.

2. Put the fillings in separate jars. Before serving, hollow out the tomatoes and stuff with the fillings.

Tartare sauce
1. Chop the capers, add a little lemon juice, the grated lemon rind and 2 tablespoons of chopped chervil.

2. Mix these ingredients into the mayonnaise. Season with salt and pepper.

Guacamole
1. Pour the remaining lemon juice into a bowl, reserving 1 teaspoonful.

2. Peel and slice the avocado. Add to the bowl with salt and pepper, a touch of Tabasco and 2 tablespoons of olive oil. Mash with a fork and mix thoroughly.

Cottage cheese with herbs
1. Mash the cottage cheese with a fork. Roughly chop 2 tablespoons of chervil and mint leaves.

2. Mix together with the teaspoon of lemon juice and 1 tablespoon of olive oil. Season with salt and pepper.

Trout paté

Preparation time:
20 min

Cooking time: 10 min

Makes 2 pots,
375 g (12 oz) each

500 g (1 lb) fillets raw or cooked trout

2 fillets smoked trout

2 bay leaves

2 thyme sprigs

2 garlic cloves, peeled

7 tablespoons white distilled vinegar

olive oil

pink peppercorns

salt, pepper

1. To cook the trout, put 2 teaspoons of salt, the bay leaves, thyme, garlic, and a few pink peppercorns into 1 litre (1¾ pints) of water and bring to the boil, then add the vinegar.

2. Boil gently for 5 minutes before adding the raw trout. With the water barely simmering, poach the fish for 5 minutes or until the flesh will part from the skin.

3. Drain off the liquid, retaining the garlic but discarding the herbs and peppercorns. Remove any remaining bones and skin from the fish.

4. Put the flesh in a food processor together with the garlic. With the processor running, add the olive oil drop by drop until a creamy consistency is obtained.

5. Mash the smoked trout fillets with a fork and add to the preparation, together with a few pink peppercorns. Season with salt and pepper.

6. Put the paté into ramekins or pots, cover with clingfilm and keep refrigerated.

TASTE BITE

SPREAD THIS PATÉ on little round rolls, or on rye bread, with spring onions, a salad leaf and a few tomato slices.

TIP

THE WHITE DISTILLED VINEGAR in this paté will allow it to keep in a refrigerator for ten days or so, but check on it each day.
This recipe can also be used for salmon or fresh and smoked mackerel.

Sunday-best chicken marinated in spices

Preparation time: 25 min

Marinade: 1 hour

Cooking time: 50 min

Serves 6

The chicken:

1 oven-ready free-range chicken, about 1.5 kg (3 lb)

4 tablespoons crème fraîche

2 tablespoons turmeric

1 teaspoon cumin

1 rosemary sprig

1 lime

1 teaspoon olive oil

salt, pepper

The sauce:

150 g (5 oz) natural yoghurt

250 g (8 oz) lemon mayonnaise

2 teaspoons turmeric

¼ teaspoon cayenne pepper

salt, pepper

1. Make a marinade with the crème fraîche, spices and 3 pinches of freshly ground pepper.

2. Put 2 tablespoons of this mixture inside the chicken with the rosemary and slices of lime.

3. Spread the rest of the marinade all over the chicken and let stand for 1 hour.

4. Pre-heat the oven to 200°C (400°F), Gas Mark 6. Drizzle the olive oil over the chicken, season it with salt and roast for about 50 minutes or until the juices run golden and clear when a skewer is inserted.

5. Remove the chicken from the oven, stand it on a plate and baste with the cooking juices, which should be nicely coloured. Let it rest for 15 minutes before carving.

6. Mix all the sauce ingredients together and season with salt and pepper.

TASTE BITE

PROVIDE LARGE SLICES of bread, a dish of sliced cucumber, some salad leaves and spring onions.

TIP

IF PREFERRED this dish can be made with chicken breast portions (one per person). To keep them moist and prevent them from shrinking, place in cold oil in a roasting pan, put in the oven and bring up to temperature in Step 4. Turn the portions over frequently and add the marinade after they have been cooking for 3 or 4 minutes.

Weekend artist's roast

Preparation time:
20 min

Cooking time: 1 hour

Serves 6

**Rolled loin of pork,
with skin removed
about 1.25 kg
(2¹/₂ lb)**

**100 g (4 oz) pitted
green olives**

olive oil

paprika

cayenne pepper

**250 g (8 oz) cream
cheese**

**1 small bunch of
fresh coriander,
coarsely chopped**

salt, pepper

1. Rinse the olives, dry them on kitchen paper and cut in half lengthways.

2. With a sharp, pointed knife make fairly deep cuts over the whole surface of the meat and push in the olives. Keep about 12 olives to add to the sauce.

3. Pre-heat the oven to 200°C (400°F), Gas Mark 6. Coat the meat with oil and sprinkle liberally with paprika and cayenne pepper to colour the surface bright orange.

4. Roast for 20 minutes in the oven at 200°C (400°F), then for a further 40 minutes at 180°C (350°F), Gas Mark 4. Check that the juices run clear when a skewer is inserted. Set aside to cool.

5. Make the sauce by mixing the rest of the olives with the cream cheese. Add the coriander and season with salt, black pepper and cayenne pepper.

TIP

TO AVOID MAKING excessively large cuts in the meat, use small olives. The dish can also be made with black or purple olives. Wait until the meat is completely cold before carving, and place it on a sheet of greaseproof paper to catch the juices.

Gardener's quiche

Preparation time:
35 min

Refrigeration:
30 min

Cooking time: 50 min

Serves 6

250 g (8 oz) ready-
made puff pastry

1 kg (2 lb) fresh
peas in pod

250 g (8 oz)
mangetout

1 egg white

1 tablespoon potato
flour

3 tablespoons
single cream

4 eggs

60 g (2½-3 oz) soft
goat's cheese

375 g (12 oz) cream
cheese

1 tablespoon
chopped chives

1 tablespoon butter

salt, pepper

TIP

THE EGG WHITE coats the pastry and prevents it from absorbing any liquid given off by the vegetables during baking. Only a small amount of egg white is used.

TASTE BITE

THIS QUICHE is the perfect accompaniment for cold meats. For the quintessential flavour of summer in the garden, add a bowl of freshly picked young broad beans, removed from the pod and boiled until tender but still firm.

1. Line a 26-cm (10-inch) flan tin with the puff pastry and refrigerate for 30 minutes.

2. Shell the peas, top and tail the mangetout and cut into strips.

3. Blanch the peas for 3 minutes in 1 litre (1¾ pints) of boiling water and the mangetout for 3 to 4 minutes. Put them into a serving bowl with the butter, mix well and set aside.

4. Whip the egg white to slacken it and brush a thin layer over the pastry. Leave it to dry.

5. Pre-heat the oven to 180°C (350°F), Gas Mark 4. Mix the potato flour with the single cream, stir over the heat for a few seconds to thicken it then transfer to a food processor. Add the eggs, goat's cheese and cream cheese and process until smooth. Season with salt and pepper.

6. Arrange the vegetables on the pastry base and pour the egg mixture over them. Sprinkle with chives.

7. Bake the quiche for about 40 minutes, until the top is domed and golden brown.

Tiger prawn and trout pies

Preparation time:
30 min

Refrigeration:
10 min

Cooking time: 25 min

Makes 6 individual pies

Ready-made puff pastry

500 g (1 lb) fresh tiger prawns, or frozen and thoroughly defrosted

200 g (7–8 oz) trout fillets

flour

5 tablespoons olive oil

3 shallots, finely chopped

1 garlic clove, crushed

1 bunch of chives, finely chopped

1 bunch of tarragon, finely chopped

250 ml (8 fl oz) flowery white wine (pinot d'Alsace)

2 tablespoons butter

cayenne pepper

1 beaten egg

salt, pepper

1. Cut the fish fillets into strips and lightly flour them.

2. Heat 1 tablespoon olive oil in a pan and fry the strips of fish, skin-side down, for 1 minute, season with salt and pepper and set aside.

3. Add the rest of the oil to the pan and cook the prawns for 3–4 minutes, stirring frequently, then season with salt and pepper and a few pinches of cayenne. Retain the oil in the pan.

4. Shell the prawns and remove the intestinal tract. Reserve the heads. Brown the shallots briefly in the retained oil. Add the prawns heads, garlic, 1 tablespoon each of the herbs, the white wine and 200 ml (7 fl oz) of water.

5. Reduce the liquid by half then pass the mixture through a sieve to produce a thick, creamy sauce. Add the butter and the rest of the herbs. Set aside to cool.

6. Pre-heat the oven to 220°C (425°F), Gas Mark 7. On a floured surface, roll out and line 6 individual tart tins with puff pastry, leaving a margin of pastry overhanging the rim. Chill in the freezer for 10 minutes.

7. Arrange the prawn tails and the strips of trout in the pastry cases. Add the herb mixture. Fold over the overhanging pastry neatly to make a lid and seal with beaten egg. Put the tarts in the oven and bake for 12 minutes.

TIP
CRAYFISH could take the place of the tiger prawns.

TASTE BITE
PLACE ANCHOVY FILLETS on any pastry that is left over. Cut into strips and baked in the oven for 5 minutes, these make excellent anchovy straws.

Cornet of shortbread 'chips' with berry ratafia

Preparation time:

The ratafia: 20 min, 5 days before

Cooking time: 10 min

The shortbread: 10 min, the day before

Cooking time: 12 min

Serves 6

For the ratafia:

500 g (1 lb) berries (blackcurrants, redcurrants, raspberries)

1 peppermint sprig

200 g (7 oz) sugar

200 ml (7 fl oz) white wine

7 tablespoons crème de cassis (blackcurrant liqueur)

For the shortbread:

125 g (4 oz) granulated sugar

1 egg

1 teaspoon grated lemon rind

150 g (5 oz) lightly salted butter, softened

250 g (8 oz) plain flour

1. Prepare the ratafia 5 days in advance. Wash the berries and drain them on kitchen paper.

2. Stir the sugar into the wine and bring to the boil. Add the berries and the mint. Bring back to the boil, lower the heat and leave to simmer gently for 5 minutes then remove from the heat and leave to soak overnight.

3. Next day, cook the mixture for 10 minutes, add the blackcurrant liqueur, discard the mint and put the mixture into pots. Cover immediately.

4. Prepare the shortbread biscuits the day before they are needed. Mix the egg with the sugar and the lemon rind in a bowl. Add the butter, then the flour, little by little.

5. Knead the pastry lightly with the tips of the fingers then roll the dough into a ball, wrap in clingfilm and place in the refrigerator.

6. The next day, pre-heat the oven to 200°C (400°F), Gas Mark 6. Roll out the pastry 1-cm ($\frac{1}{2}$-inch) thick and cut into fingers the size of large chips.

7. Bake for 10 to 12 minutes on a non-stick or greased baking tray. Leave to cool completely on a wire tray before dredging with sugar and storing in an airtight tin.

TASTE BITE

ALSO GOOD with a coulis of red soft fruits or fromage blanc.

TIP

RATAFIA is a sweet liqueur made with fruits soaked in eau-de-vie. This version is based on it but, unlike that made to the traditional recipe, it will not keep for more than 3 weeks in a refrigerator.

Cherry clafoutis

Preparation time:
25 min

Cooking time: 45 min

Serves 6

750 g (1¹/₂ lb) black cherries

5 eggs

100 g (3¹/₂ oz) caster sugar

4 tablespoons flour

150 ml (¹/₄ pint) single cream

7 tablespoons milk

1 teaspoon grated lemon rind

1 tablespoon rum

1 tablespoon butter

salt

1. Pre-heat the oven to 180° (350°F), Gas Mark 4. Remove the cherry stalks but leave the stones.

2. Whisk the eggs with the sugar and a pinch of salt. Add the flour and continue whisking while incorporating the cream and the milk.

3. Add the lemon rind and rum.

4. Butter a glazed shallow ovenproof dish and place the cherries in it in a closely packed layer. Pour the batter over them.

5. Bake the clafoutis for about 45 minutes, topping with a few dabs of butter halfway through the cooking time.

6. Dust the clafoutis with caster sugar and allow to cool.

 TIP

YOU CAN ALSO MAKE individual clafoutis in small baking dishes. Use 10 to 12 cherries for each and pack them in the picnic basket still in their dishes. A variation on this recipe replaces the cream and milk with 250 g (8 oz) of ricotta cheese.

TASTE BITE

THE MORE CHERRIES, the tastier the clafoutis. Cooking the cherries with the stones in gives them a delicious flavour but don't forget to warn guests about the risk to their teeth!

Semolina gateau with nectarines

Preparation time:
35 min

Cooking time: 45 min

Serves 6

4 nectarines

200 g (7 oz) sugar

3 cardamom seeds

½ litre (17 fl oz) milk

1 cinnamon stick

**grated rind of
1 orange and
1 lemon**

75 g (3 oz) fine semolina

2 tablespoons rum

2 eggs, beaten

1. Peel the nectarines, Cook for 5 minutes over low heat, in a syrup made by boiling 100 g (3½ oz) of sugar with 7 tablespoons of water. Drain, and leave to cool.

2. Put 50 g (2 oz) sugar and 3½ tablespoons water in a flan dish and cook over fierce heat until it turns to a fairly dark caramel. Remove from the heat and tilt the dish until the sides are coated then leave to get cold.

3. Put the milk into a saucepan. Open the cardamoms and scrape the aromatic black seeds into the milk. Add the cinnamon stick and citrus rinds and bring to the boil.

4. Pour in the semolina, stirring continuously. Add the remaining sugar and cook for 2 minutes, stirring constantly, before adding the rum.

5. Remove the semolina from the heat, leave to cool for 2 minutes, remove the cinnamon stick, stir in the well-beaten eggs and the nectarine segments.

6. Pre-heat the oven to 180°C (350°F), Gas Mark 4. Pour the prepared mixture into the caramel-coated dish and bake for 45 minutes. Allow to cool before turning the gateau out of the dish.

TASTE BITE

EXCELLENT with a fresh fruit salad (nectarines, apricots, raspberries, melon) and small, crisp biscuits.

Terrine of pork cooked in cider

Preparation time:
25 min, the day
before

Refrigeration:
12 hours

Cooking time:
3 hours

Serves 6

1.5 kg (3 lb) leg of pork

1 sachet (11 g) gelatine

1 lemon

375 g (12 oz) onions, peeled and sliced

3 tablespoons groundnut oil

2 tablespoons wine vinegar

450 ml ($^3/_4$ pint) cider

$^1/_2$ tablespoon allspice

2 cloves

5–6 peppercorns

2 bay leaves

3 garlic cloves, peeled

salt

1. Remove the skin from the pork and season the meat with salt.

2. Cut a thin layer of rind from the lemon and blanch it for 10 minutes in boiling water.

3. Brown the pork on all sides for 10 minutes in oil in a cast-iron casserole on the hob then remove and set aside. Brown the onions in the same oil.

4. Pre-heat the oven to 150°C (300°F), Gas Mark 2. Replace the pork in the casserole and add the vinegar and all but $3^1/_2$ tablespoons of the cider. Add the spices, bay leaves, garlic and lemon rind.

5. Cover and cook in the oven for about $2^3/_4$ hours (see TIP) then add the remaining cider.

6. Drain the meat, discarding only the spices and bay leaves, and reserve the liquid. When the pork has cooled, remove the bone and cut the meat into small cubes.

7. Measure the reserved liquid into a pan over a low heat and sprinkle over sufficient gelatine to set the quantity of liquid according to the manufacturer's instructions. Whisk to dissolve completely. Do not allow to boil. Cool until beginning to thicken.

8. Stir in the meat cubes, onions and garlic. Put into a terrine, cover with foil-wrapped card and a weight. Refrigerate for 12 hours.

TASTE BITE

EXCELLENT SLICED and served with onion preserve or gherkins. Leg of pork is also delicious cooked whole, then sliced when cold.

TIP

TO ENSURE THAT THE PORK is cooked through, turn it at regular intervals throughout the cooking period. It is done when the juices run clear after a thin, sharp skewer is inserted well into the meat.

punting

along

a river

Mussels, prawns and haricot bean salad

Preparation time:
40 min,

overnight soaking

Cooking time:
1³/₄ hours

Serves 6

750 g (1¹/₂ lb) mussels

300 g (10 oz) dried haricot beans, soaked overnight

2 onions, peeled and sliced

1 carrot, peeled and sliced

1 celery stick, sliced

1 bouquet garni

7 tablespoons dry white wine

1 large pink shallot

1 bunch of flat-leaf parsley

1 teaspoon cider vinegar

2 tablespoons olive oil

200 g (7 oz) small cooked prawns

salt, pepper

1. Drain the beans, put into a saucepan, cover with cold water. Add the onions, carrot, celery and bouquet garni and bring to the boil. Boil rapidly for 10 minutes

2. Boil the beans for a further 1–1¹/₂ hours or until tender. They should be soft but unbroken. Discard the vegetables and bouquet garni and season with salt and pepper.

3. Scrub the mussels, removing the beards and discarding any open shells, put into a saucepan with the white wine, cover tightly and place over a high heat. As soon as they open, remove from the heat and strain the cooking liquor into a basin, through a fine-mesh sieve. Shell the mussels, discarding any that remain shut.

4. For the vinaigrette, peel and chop the shallot and coarsely chop the parsley. Mash a few of the beans to a paste and stir this into the mussel liquor. Add the cider vinegar, shallot, parsley and olive oil and season with salt pepper. Coat the beans with this dressing, add the shellfish and refrigerate in an airtight container until needed.

TASTE BITE

DELICIOUS when the seasoning is just right. If the beans absorb some of the vinaigrette as they cool, don't hesitate to add extra salt and pepper and perhaps a touch of vinegar.

TIP

TINNED HARICOT BEANS may be used instead of dried. This kind of salad also goes well with smoked fish.

Buckwheat pancakes with salami

Preparation time:
10 min, the day
before

Cooking time: 20 min

Serves 6

250 g (8 oz) salami, thinly sliced

100 g (3¹/₂ oz) buckwheat flour

2 tablespoons olive oil

250 ml (8 fl oz) carbonated mineral water

1 tablespoon groundnut oil

75 g (3 oz) lightly salted butter

salt, pepper

1. Prepare the dough for the pancakes the previous day. Put the flour into a mixing bowl with the salt, olive oil and mineral water.

2. Mix together and knead until it is smooth but do not let it become elastic. Set aside in the refrigerator.

3. The next day, divide the dough into 6 and roll out thin pancakes. Cook, one at a time, in a hot, oiled frying pan of medium size. Put a piece of butter the size of a hazelnut on each.

4. Remove any skin from around the edges of the salami. Put a layer of salami slices on the pancakes, roll them up and cut into rings.

5. Secure with a cocktail stick to prevent them unwinding and store in an airtight container.

☀ TIP

MAKE TWO OR THREE TIMES the amount if you intend serving these pancakes with other dishes, such as cold meats, or marinated fish (see recipe for Mackerel Fillets with Redcurrants on page 38) in the course of the picnic.

Crab with vinaigrette

Preparation time:
1 hour

Needs no cooking

Serves 4

6 cooked crabs

2 white shallots

**2 tablespoons
lemon juice**

**4 pinches cayenne
pepper**

**4 tablespoons
mayonnaise**

**2 tablespoons
chopped parsley**

**1 teaspoon chopped
dill**

2 gherkins

salt, pepper

1. Crack the large crab claws and the legs with nutcrackers and remove the meat.

2. Halve the body sections and pick out the white meat from the leg sockets. Scrape the dark meat from the shells then select 4 for the presentation and clean them thoroughly. Check the claw meat carefully for pieces of shell then set aside.

3. Peel and chop the shallots and mix with the crab meat. Add the lemon juice, cayenne pepper, mayonnaise and herbs, season with salt and pepper and keep cool.

4. Slice the gherkins. Fill the 4 prepared shells with the crab mixture and garnish with the gherkin rings.

TIP

IF PREFERRED, buy dressed crabs from a good fish-monger.

TASTE BITE

SERVE with a tomato and cucumber salad.

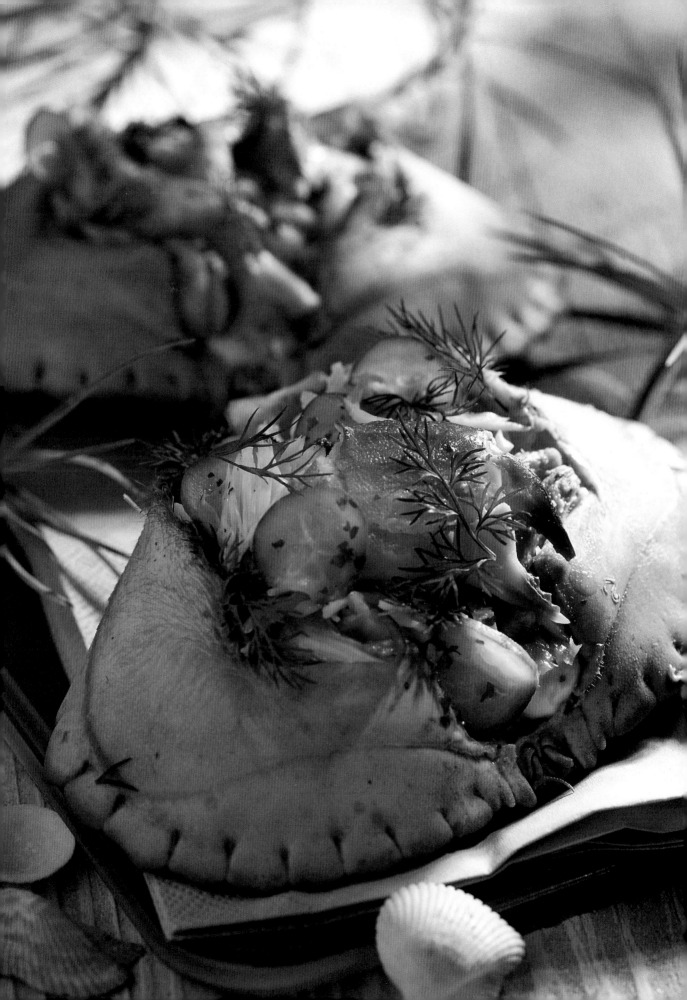

King prawn tails with green mayonnaise

Preparation time:
30 min

Marinade: 2 hours

Cooking time: 35 min

Serves 6

TASTE BITE
EXCELLENT on buttered slices of rye bread with small boiled potatoes (see illustration).

TIP

THE GRAPESEED OIL stabilises the emulsion and prevents the mayonnaise from separating due to the warmth in the atmosphere. If using pre-prepared may-onnaise, add tarragon to it.

For the king prawn tails:

24 king prawn tails

$\frac{1}{2}$ bottle dry white wine

1 celery stick, chopped

1 tablespoon grated fresh ginger

1 bay leaf

1 thyme sprig

1 lemon

salt, pepper

For the mayonnaise:

1 egg yolk

200 ml (7 fl oz) grapeseed oil

1 tablespoon chopped tarragon

1 tablespoon chopped parsley

1 tablespoon chopped chervil

salt, pepper

1. Remove the shells and heads from the prawn tails and the black intestinal thread along the back. Rinse and pat dry with kitchen paper.

2. Make a light stock from 900 ml (1$\frac{1}{2}$ pints) water, wine, celery, ginger, bay leaf, thyme and 2 tablespoons lemon juice. Bring to the boil and simmer for 30 minutes, then strain.

3. Bring the stock to the boil, lower the heat, add the prawn tails and boil gently for 5 minutes or until cooked through, then drain and allow to cool.

4. To make the mayonnaise, put the egg yolk in a basin, add 2 good pinches of salt and beat with a balloon whisk. When it begins to thicken start adding the oil, a few drops at a time. If it remains liquid, continue stirring vigorously; the success of the mayonnaise depends on this early stage. Slowly drizzle in grapeseed oil until the mayonnaise has reached the required consistency. If it is too thick add a little water and a touch of lemon juice to enhance the flavour

5. Season with pepper, stir in the herbs and set aside.

6. Pack the king prawn tails in the picnic basket in a separate container from the mayonnaise, and take along a supply of cocktail sticks.

Sardines in a spicy sauce with bread and red butter

Preparation time:
30 min

Marinade: 4 hours

Cooking time: 15 min

Serves 6

12 fresh sardines

5 tablespoons olive oil

2 shallots, peeled and chopped

2 garlic cloves, peeled and chopped

1/2 chilli

150 ml (1/4 pint) white wine

150 ml (1/4 pint) cider vinegar

1 bay leaf

2 teaspoons coriander seed

salt

For the red butter:

125 g (4 oz) butter

1 shallot, peeled and chopped

4 tablespoons lemon juice

1 tablespoon paprika

2 pinches cayenne pepper

salt

1. Scale and wash the sardines, dry them and remove the heads.

2. Open the fish and detach the fillets from the backbone, rinse them and pat dry.

3. Heat the olive oil in a frying pan and add the sardines, skin side down, and seal for 30 seconds. Remove from the heat and leave the oil in the pan.

4. Lay the sardines, head to tail, in an earthenware dish.

5. Fry the shallots and garlic gently in the remaining oil. Add the chilli, white wine, vinegar, bay leaf and coriander seeds and boil vigorously to reduce by one quarter. Leave to cool for one minute before pouring it over the sardines. Leave in a cool place for 4 hours.

6. For the red butter: mix the paprika and cayenne pepper into the softened butter, adding the lemon juice gradually, and beat well. Add the chopped shallot and a pinch of salt. Put the butter mixture into a pot and store in a cool place.

TIP

FOR SOMETHING in a similar vein, take a tin of sardines in olive oil and mash with some butter, add a few drops of lemon juice, a pinch of cayenne pepper and a little chopped shallot. While not very pretty, this 'paté' is delicious spread on crusty bread. Make a little pot of it especially for those who are hooked on the flavour!

Potato and taramasalata pancakes

Preparation time:
35 min

Cooking time: 35 min

Serves 6

For the taramasalata:

150 g (5 oz) smoked cod roe

2 tablespoons lemon juice

handful stale white breadcrumbs

250 ml (8 fl oz) crème fraîche

grapeseed oil

salt, pepper

For the pancakes:

300 g (10 oz) salad potatoes, peeled

1 courgette, grated

3 tablespoons flour

3 tablespoons crème fraîche

3 eggs

1 pinch grated nutmeg

1. To prepare the taramasalata, remove the fine membrane from the cod roes and put them into a food processor, together with the lemon juice, breadcrumbs and crème fraîche. Alternatively, beat together with a balloon whisk.

2. With the processor running, gradually add the oil until a creamy consistency is reached. Correct the seasoning and set aside.

3. To prepare the pancakes: cook the potatoes for 15 minutes in boiling water, add the grated courgette and cook for a further 5 minutes then drain.

4. While the potatoes and courgettes are still hot, mash them with a fork. Stir in the flour and crème fraîche and add the 3 eggs, one at a time, but take care not to over-mix. Season with the nutmeg and form into pancake circles.

5. Cook the pancakes by dropping the pancake circles onto a large, non-stick frying pan. Place them in an airtight container and serve them with the taramasalata.

TIP
TARAMASALATA made with smoked cod roe is very pale because it contains no colouring matter.

TASTE BITE
GOOD WITH A SQUEEZE OF LEMON. Stack the pancakes after the style of a club sandwich, adding smoked salmon, sprigs of dill and sliced cucumber.

Mackerel fillets with redcurrants

Preparation time:
25 min

Marinade: 1 hour

Cooking time:
30 min

Serves 6

6 unsweetened pancakes or wraps

3 mackerel, weighing 350 g (12 oz) each or 6 pre-packed fillets

200 g (7 oz) redcurrants

1 tablespoon balsamic vinegar

1 tablespoon grated fresh ginger

1 tablespoon soy sauce

1 tablespoon olive oil

1 onion

3–4 pieces of sun-dried tomato in olive oil, finely chopped

pepper

1. Get the fishmonger to fillet the mackerel. Lay the fillets in a dish, skin side down.

2. Squeeze the juice from 125 g (4 oz) of the redcurrants by crushing them by hand. Keep the rest of the berries to garnish the fillets.

3. Add the balsamic vinegar, grated ginger and soy sauce to the redcurrant juice.

4. Pour this over the fillets and leave to marinate for 1 hour in a cool place.

5. Drain and reserve the marinade. Pat the fillets dry with kitchen paper and slice into 2.5-cm (1-inch) wide strips.

6. Heat some oil in a frying pan and add the mackerel strips, cut side down, for a few seconds, then salt lightly and season with pepper. Pour in the marinade and leave to cook for a few more seconds then remove from the heat.

7. Pack the fillets in a container with the onion, cut in rings, and the pieces of sun-dried tomato. To serve, wrap the mixture in the pancakes or wraps and garnish with the reserved redcurrants.

TIP

IF SERVING these as part of an outdoor meal in the garden, they could be presented in the form of mini-pizzas. Cut 6 circles of puff pastry and spread with tomato pizza sauce and pieces of raw mackerel. Bake in a very hot oven for three minutes.

Brittany plum and apple pudding

Preparation time:
20 min

Cooking time: 45 min

Serves 6

125 g (4oz) sugar

4 eggs

200 g (7 oz) plain flour

125 g (4 oz) melted butter

2 tablespoons rum

400 ml (14 fl oz) full-cream milk

2 Braeburn apples, peeled and grated

400 g (13 oz) purple plums, halved and stoned

1 tablespoon caster sugar

1. Pre-heat the oven to 200°C (400°F), Gas Mark 6. Whisk the eggs and sugar together until white and foamy.

2. Continue whisking while adding the flour to prevent lumps forming. Add the melted butter and the rum.

3. Slowly add the milk, stirring constantly, to obtain a thin batter.

4. Add the apple and plum halves to the batter.

5. Pour the mixture into a buttered, heatproof dish and bake for 35 minutes, then turn up the heat to 220°C (425°F), Gas Mark 7 and leave to cook for a further 10 minutes to brown the top, but check after 5 minutes to make sure it is not over-browning.

 TIP

THE APPLES give a touch of acidity and improve the appearance of the pudding.

⦿ TASTE BITE

VERY GOOD with straw-berries or an assortment of fruit, such as apples, peaches and strawberries, threaded on skewers with mint leaves.

Club sandwich
(Salmon, avocados, prawns, Cheddar cheese)

Preparation time:
30 min

Needs no cooking

Serves 6

12 slices white bread

12 slices wholemeal bread

2 avocados

4 tablespoons lemon juice

125 g (4 oz) smoked salmon

50 g (2 oz) cream cheese

150 g (5 oz) cooked, peeled prawns

12 thin slices Cheddar cheese

6 dill sprigs

1 bunch of chervil

6 lettuce leaves

6 teaspoons plum chutney

salt, pepper

skewers

 TIP

A LITTLE BUTTER spread on the bread prevents it from drying out. If plum chutney is unavailable substitute plum jam sharpened with vinegar.

1. Toast the bread slices.

2. Peel and slice the avocados and sprinkle with lemon juice to prevent them discolouring. Season with salt and pepper.

3. Assemble the sandwiches alternating brown and white bread and using 4 slices per sandwich. Put a little cream cheese with the smoked salmon; a squeeze of lemon and dill sprigs with the prawns; sprigs of chervil, avocado slices, lettuce and plum chutney with the Cheddar.

4. Stack the sandwiches in a pile and cut them in half. Secure with a skewer through the centre, wrap them in foil and store in an airtight container.

Haddock and herring snack

Preparation time:
15 min

Cooking time: 20 min

Serves 6

**300 g (10 oz)
smoked haddock
fillets with skin
(not colour-stained
fillets)**

**4 sweet-cured
herrings**

**12 small salad
potatoes**

**2 white onions,
peeled and finely
chopped**

**3¹/₂ tablespoons
white wine**

**1 tablespoon
sherry vinegar**

**3 tablespoons
groundnut oil**

**1 teaspoon grated
fresh ginger**

**2 tablespoons
chopped chives**

salt, pepper

1. Cook the potatoes in their skins for 10 to 15 minutes in boiling, salted water.

2. Lay the haddock flat and with a knife blade held on the slant, cut into very thin slices. Cut the herring slices in four.

3. Drain the potatoes, skin them and cut into rings. Make a dressing with the white wine, sherry vinegar and oil and mix well with the potatoes and chopped onion.

4. Add the fish to the potato salad, together with the ginger and chives. Season with pepper and keep in a cool place.

 TASTE BITE

GOOD made into sand-wiches with little toasted sesame seed rolls.

TIP

IN THIS DISH the haddock is left raw. If, however, you should find it too salty (this is governed by the quality of the fish) marinate it for 1 hour before use in a little lemon juice or white wine.

Cold lamb and mint sauce on an open sandwich

Preparation time: 25 min

Cooking time: 30 min

Serves 6

750 g (1¹/₂ lb) leg of lamb, boned and rolled

1 tablespoon butter

1 tablespoon ras-el-hanout (see under Step 5)

1 bunch of mint

200 ml crème fraîche

1 loaf rough country bread

1 handful young spinach shoots

sea salt

salt, pepper

1. Pre-heat the oven to 200°C (400°F), Gas Mark 6.

2. Melt the butter and mix with the ras-al-hanout, season with salt and pepper. Coat the lamb all over with this flavoured butter.

3. Brown the meat on all sides in a frying pan then put it into a roasting tin, and baste with any remaining flavoured butter. Roast for 25–30 minutes in the oven then leave to cool for 15 minutes. If the meat is to be well done, make sure the juices run clear when a skewer is inserted.

4. Finely chop the mint leaves and season with salt and pepper, then add the crème fraîche. Slice the bread and toast it. Wash and dry the spinach shoots.

5. Carve the cold lamb and lay slices on the toast. Garnish with the spinach shoots and serve it with the mint sauce and a sprinkle of sea salt.

(Ras-al-hanout is an exotic and complex blend of numerous spices including cloves, cinnamon, nutmeg, cardamon and peppercorns used in Moroccan and Tunisian cuisine. Search for it in delicatessens)

Stilton and Cheddar terrine with bacon

Preparation time: 25 min

Refrigeration: 2 hours

Needs no cooking

Serves 6

200 g (7 oz) Stilton

100 g (3¹/₂ oz) butter

2 tablespoons brandy

150 g (5 oz) Cheddar

2 tablespoons crème fraîche

50 g (2 oz) shelled pistachio nuts

8 slices bacon, lightly grilled

pepper

1. Mash the Stilton and butter together with a fork to make a smooth paste with brandy to taste and a little black pepper.

2. Cut the Cheddar into pieces and put in a food processor with 1 tablespoon crème fraîche and blend thoroughly. Add a little more crème fraîche if necessary to obtain a spreadable paste.

3. Roughly chop the pistachios in the food processor. Line a rectangular terrine with clingfilm and spread a layer of creamed Stilton over the base. Cover with slices of bacon and some of the chopped pistachios. Add a layer of creamed Cheddar, then more bacon and nuts. Continue with the layers until all the ingredients are used up. Cover with foil-wrapped card and a weight. Refrigerate for 2 hours before using.

TASTE BITE
SLICE AND SERVE with poppy seed rolls.

TIP
STILTON is a medium blue-veined cheese with a brushed rind and a very pronounced flavour. Cheddar is a pressed cheese with a natural rind. Avoid the factory-made varieties if possible.

Chicken pie

Preparation time:
45 min

Cooking time: 1 hour

Serves 6

**500 g (1 lb) diced
lean pork**

50 g (2 oz) butter

**chicken legs
weighing 625 g
(1¹/₄ lb)**

**4 onions, peeled
and sliced**

**250 g (8 oz) button
mushrooms, chopped**

**300 ml (¹/₂ pint)
sherry**

**2 pinches of
tandoori spice**

**2 pinches of mixed
spice**

**1 kg (2 lb) green
asparagus**

**shortcrust pastry,
rolled into
2 circles to fit
pie tin**

salt

*Note: If preferred use half
pork and half veal*

1. Gently fry the diced pork for 5 minutes in half the butter. Brown the chicken for 10 minutes in the same pan, adding the onions halfway through.

2. Remove the chicken and onions from the pan, add the mushrooms and the rest of the butter and brown for 2 minutes. Put the meat and vegetables into a cast iron casserole.

3. Swill the pan with 250 ml (8 fl oz) of sherry and pour over the meat. Add the 2 spices, cover and cook on the hob for 20 minutes.

4. Cut off the tough stems of the asparagus and cook the tips for 10 minutes in boiling salted water then drain.

5. Remove the meat from the pot, skin and bone the chicken and cut into cubes.

6. Drain the rest of the ingredients, blend the meat, mushrooms and cooking liquor in the food processor, then transfer to a mixing bowl and stir in the diced chicken, asparagus and the remaining sherry.

7. Pre-heat the oven to 200°C (400°F), Gas Mark 6. Line a non-stick pie tin with one circle of pastry. Pile on the prepared mixture, cover with the second circle of pastry and seal the edges. Make a couple of cuts in the lid to allow the steam to escape. Bake for 30 minutes.

Apple crumble with mango

Preparation time:
25 min, 1 hour in
advance

Cooking time: 40 min

Serves 6

6 dessert apples

1 ripe mango

65 g (2¹/₂ oz) raisins

2 tablespoons rum

**125 g (4 oz) plain
flour**

**160 g (5¹/₂ oz)
softened butter**

**100 g (3¹/₂ oz) brown
sugar**

1 cinnamon stick

1 pinch salt

1. Soak the raisins in the rum until they are swollen.

2. Put the flour, salt and 65 g (2¹/₂ oz) brown sugar in a mixing bowl. Rub in 125 g (4 oz) butter with the fingertips to the consistency of coarse breadcrumbs and leave to chill for 1 hour.

3. Peel and core the apples. Peel the mango and remove the stone. Cut the fruit into pieces.

4. Cook the fruit for 15 to 20 minutes in a large frying pan with 30 g (1 oz) of butter, the remaining brown sugar and the cinnamon stick. Stir frequently until the apples are squashy and the juice that ran from the mango has evaporated. Add the drained raisins.

5. Pre-heat the oven to 220°C (425°F), Gas Mark 7. Lightly butter a gratin dish.

6. Remove the cinnamon stick and arrange the fruit in the dish. Spread the crumble mixture over it. Bake for 20 minutes until the crust is golden and crisp.

TASTE BITE

GOOD served with whipped cream – remember to pack an aerosol of whipped cream in the hamper.

TIP

THE EASIEST METHOD of carrying the crumble to the picnic is to leave it in the baking dish. One lucky person gets to scrape out the crusty bits left in the dish!

Cake flavoured with citrus rind

Preparation time:
25 min

Soaking time: 1 hour

Cooking time: 45 min

Serves 6

100 g (3¹/₂ oz) lemon and candied orange rind

3 tablespoons rum

200 g (7 oz) plain flour

1 teaspoon baking powder

150 g (5 oz) softened butter

100 g (3¹/₂ oz) sugar

3 eggs

salt

1. Cut up the citrus rinds with scissors and put them to soak for 1 hour in the rum.

2. Pre-heat the oven to 180°C (350°F), Gas Mark 4. Sift the flour with the baking powder. Beat the butter and sugar together to a creamy consistency in a mixing bowl. Beat in the eggs one at a time, then the flour. When a smooth mixture is obtained, add the rinds and the rum.

3. Pour the mixture into a non-stick cake tin and bake for 45 minutes. When the top has formed a dome, raise the heat to 200°C (400°F), Gas Mark 6 to finish browning the cake but take care it doesn't burn.

TASTE BITE
SERVE WARM OR COLD with tea laced with whisky, brought along in a thermos flask.

TIP
RAISINS SOAKED in rum could be substituted for the citrus rind.

beaches
and sand
dunes

Aubergine, ricotta cheese and ham rolls

Preparation time:
25 min

Cooking time: 40 min

Serves 6

6 small ciabatta loaves, or any large crusty rolls

6 small aubergines

1 chopped garlic clove

8 tablespoons olive oil

300 g (10 oz) ricotta cheese

1 tablespoon balsamic vinegar

1 tablespoon chopped mint

1 tablespoon chopped basil plus extra leaves

1 tablespoon chopped parsley

6 tomatoes

6 slices Parma ham

1 sun-dried tomato in olive oil, finely chopped

salt, pepper

1. Pre-heat the oven to 200°C (400°F), Gas Mark 6. Make an incision around the stem end of the aubergines, place them on the centre oven shelf and cook for 40 minutes until the skins are shrivelled. Allow them to cool then cut in half, scoop out the pulp and season it with salt and pepper.

2. Add the chopped garlic to the aubergine pulp and whisk the mixture while slowly adding 4–6 tablespoons of olive oil to obtain a creamy consistency. Set aside in a cool place.

3. Mash the ricotta with a fork. Add the balsamic vinegar and 2 tablespoons of olive oil. Season with salt and pepper.

4. Mix the chopped mint, parsley and basil into the ricotta cheese.

5. Slice the tomatoes in half, remove the cores and seeds and cut the flesh into cubes.

6. Split the loaves or rolls in half and spread with the fillings, combining half the ricotta with the sun-dried tomato; the remaining ricotta with slices of Parma ham; and the aubergine with the diced fresh tomatoes and the whole basil leaves torn into strips.

TIP

FOCACCIA, or any other flatbread, can also be used.

Egg-filled rolls

Preparation time:
25 min

Needs no cooking

Serves 6

 TIP

A MORE LUXURIOUS SNACK can be made by spreading tapenade (see page 125) on the bread and garnishing with marinated raw fish fillets, such as sardines and Mackerel with Redcurrants (see page 38), or even with salamis.

6 round, flat bread rolls

2 small green peppers

4 tomatoes

3 hard-boiled eggs

bunch of spring onions

1 large garlic clove

1 teaspoon vinegar

3 tablespoons olive oil

100 g (3¹/₂ oz) assorted salad leaves (rocket, winter chicory, chervil)

12 anchovy fillets

24 pitted black olives

2 basil sprigs

salt, pepper

1. Char the skins of the peppers until they blister, either over a gas flame or under a hot grill. Put in a plastic bag for 5 minutes to loosen the skins further and then peel and slice them.

2. Slice the tomatoes, shell the eggs and slice into rounds. Slice the spring onions and peel the garlic.

3. Split the bread rolls in half and discard some of the soft crumb. Rub the inside surfaces with the garlic.

4. Mix the vinegar and olive oil and season with salt and pepper. Sprinkle a few drops over the insides of the rolls. Arrange the salad leaves, spring onions, peppers, tomatoes and egg slices on the bottom halves. Top with the anchovies, olives and torn basil leaves. Sprinkle on the rest of the oil and vinegar.

5. Cover with the top halves of the rolls and wrap in clingfilm.

Catalan-style bread with marinated sea bass

Preparation time:
30 min

Marinade: 1 hour

Needs no cooking

Serves 6

**1 sea bass fillet,
500-600 g (1–1¼ lb)**

**12 large slices
rough country bread**

1 lime

3 spring onions

1 chilli

**2 sprigs of fennel
leaf or dill,
coarsely chopped**

3 ripe tomatoes

olive oil

salt, pepper

1. For the marinade: cut the sea bass in strips, squeeze the juice from the lime and chop the spring onions. Deseed the chilli and cut into rings.

2. Sprinkle the lime juice over the fish. Strew with the chilli, spring onions and fennel or dill. Cover with clingfilm and set aside for 1 hour in a cool place.

3. Cut a tomato in half and rub it over the slices of bread so that the pulp seeps in. Season with salt and pepper and a drizzle of olive oil.

4. Drain the fish and season it with salt and several twists of the pepper mill.

5. Arrange the strips of sea bass on the bread slices, alternating with tomato slices.

◉ TASTE BITE

IF YOU LEAVE the preparation of the bread until the last minute, you will be rewarded with the fruity aromas of the tomato pulp and the olive oil.

💡 TIP

THIS RECIPE is based on *ceviche* – the South American dish of raw fish marinated in citrus juice, usually lime. Sea bream or tuna can replace sea bass. Whatever kind of fish is used, it must be super-fresh.

Olive and thyme bread

Preparation time:
25 min, 1 hour
in advance

Cooking time: 55 min

Serves 6–8

For the dough:

500 g (1 lb) plain flour

**40 g (1½ oz) baker's yeast
(if using dried yeast, follow maker's instructions)**

2 teaspoons sugar

1 teaspoon salt

4 tablespoons olive oil

For the topping:

1.5 kg (3 lb) onions, peeled and finely chopped

1 teaspoon sugar

2 thyme sprigs

16 pitted black olives

16 anchovies in oil (optional)

3½ tablespoons olive oil

salt, pepper

1. For the bread dough: in a small bowl, stir the yeast into 300 ml (½ pint) of warm water. Sift the flour with the sugar and salt into a mixing bowl and make a well in the centre.

2. Pour the olive oil and the dissolved yeast into the well and incorporate the flour by hand, kneading the dough until it forms a smooth ball. Leave to rest for 1 hour in a cool place.

3. For the topping: heat the oil in a heavy-based pan and sweat the onions, covered, over a low heat, until all the liquid from them has evaporated (about 30 minutes).

4. Sprinkle the softened onions with the sugar, season with salt and cook gently uncovered for about 10 minutes to colour slightly. Rub the thyme and add the leaves to the onion.

5. Pre-heat the oven to 200°C (400°F), Gas Mark 6. Oil a baking sheet or pizza tray. Flour the work surface and roll out the dough to a thickness of 5 mm (¼ inch).

6. Lay the dough on the baking sheet and raise a border all round. Leave to rise for 15 minutes at room temperature then top with the onions, anchovy fillets and black olives. Bake in the oven for 15–20 minutes, until the edges are browned.

TIP

IF YOU USE dried yeast in place of baker's yeast, leave the dough to rise for longer than indicated on the packet. You could also make this dish with a ready-prepared pizza base.

Red mullet and sweet pepper flan

Preparation time:
35 min

Cooking time: 30 min

Serves 6

**6 red mullet,
filleted**

**2 red onions,
peeled and chopped**

**3 small yellow
peppers**

**1 garlic clove,
peeled and crushed**

**300 g (10 oz) puff
pastry**

**1 tablespoon
chopped chives**

1 tablespoon butter

**3 tablespoons olive
oil**

sea salt, pepper

1. Check the fillets for any bones that have been overlooked before placing the fish in a cool place.

2. Soften the onions for 20 minutes in 2 tablespoons of olive oil. Leave aside to cool.

3. Char the peppers over a gas flame or under a hot grill, then place in a plastic bag for 5 minutes to let the steam loosen the skins. Peel and crush the garlic.

4. Peel and deseed the peppers. Cut the flesh into strips and put in a dish to marinate with the garlic and 1 tablespoon of olive oil.

5. Pre-heat the oven to 200°C (400°F), Gas Mark 6. Grease a baking sheet. Roll out the pastry into a rectangle about 40 x 15 cm (16 x 6 inches) and place on the baking sheet. Turn up a border all round it.

6. Cut the fish into strips. Cover the pastry with the onion, the strips of fish and peppers, reserving two or three strips of pepper for the garnish. Bake for 10 minutes.

7. Chop the reserved strips of pepper into small dice and scatter over the flan with the chives. Season with a few grains of sea salt and pepper.

-☼- TIP

FROZEN FILLETS can be used equally well for this dish.

Assortment of crudités with anchovy, tuna, goat's cheese and prawn sauces

Preparation time:
1 hour

No cooking needed

Serves 6

A good assortment of raw vegetables:

tomatoes, carrots, fennel, small artichokes, button mushrooms, celery, black radishes, spring onions, cucumber, red, yellow and green peppers

For the prawn sauce:

100 g (3½ oz) cooked, peeled prawns

100 g (3½ oz) cottage cheese

7 tablespoons crème fraîche

2 tablespoons lemon juice

1 tablespoon tomato ketchup

1 teaspoon soy sauce

3 tablespoons olive oil

½ clove garlic

salt, pepper

For the anchovy sauce:

12 anchovy fillets

4 garlic cloves, peeled

2 tablespoons lemon juice

2 tablespoons olive oil

pepper

For the tuna sauce:

150 g (5 oz) canned tuna in olive oil

4 tablespoons capers

2 tablespoons lemon juice

200 g (7 oz) cottage cheese

1 tablespoon coarsely chopped parsley and chives

1 teaspoon curry powder

salt, pepper

Goat's cheese sauce:

200 g (7 oz) cottage cheese

2 small round goat's milk cheeses

1 teaspoon balsamic vinegar

1 tablespoon chopped basil

salt, pepper

1. Scrape the carrots, cut them into long strips and cover with clingfilm.

2. Trim the root from the radishes. Leave the other vegetables whole.

3. Prepare the sauces as described below and store in jars.

4. Blend the prawns to a creamy consistency with the other ingredients for this sauce. Season with salt and pepper.

5. Blend the anchovies, garlic, 1 teaspoon of water and the lemon juice in a food processor, and slowly add the olive oil, a little at a time. Season with pepper.

6. Drain the tuna and blend it in a food processor with the capers and lemon juice, or mash with a fork. Mix in the cottage cheese, herbs and curry powder. Season with salt and pepper.

7. Blend the goat's cheese with the cottage cheese and balsamic vinegar in a food processor, or mash with a fork. Add the basil, mix well and season with salt and pepper.

Terrine Niçoise

Preparation time:
25 min

Cooking time: 30 min

Serves 6

**300 g (10 oz) salad
potatoes, peeled**

75 g (3 oz) butter

**250 g (8 oz) fine
green beans**

**6 quail's eggs or
3 hard-boiled eggs,
halved**

**400-g (13-oz) can
tuna in brine**

**150 g (5 oz) natural
yogurt**

**2 tablespoons lemon
juice**

**8 basil leaves, torn
into pieces**

salt, pepper

1. Boil the potatoes for 20 minutes in salted water then drain and mash with a fork, together with the butter.

2. Top and tail the green beans and cook them for 6 to 8 minutes in boiling salted water, keeping them slightly crisp. Drain thoroughly.

3. Boil the quail's eggs for 3 minutes and cool in cold water before shelling.

4. Drain the tuna and stir it into the mashed potato, add the yogurt and mix thoroughly to a smooth paste. Add the lemon juice and basil and season with salt and pepper.

5. Line a terrine or a rectangular mould with clingfilm. Put a layer of beans in the base and pour half the tuna mixture over them. Place the quail's eggs in a single line down the centre, pressing them in slightly. Cover with the rest of the tuna mixture and finish with another layer of beans.

6. Cover with foil-wrapped card and a weight. Keep refrigerated until required.

TASTE BITE
SERVE WITH CHERRY TOMATOES and either tapenade (see page 125) or mayonnaise

TIP
THE CLINGFILM LINING makes it easier to turn the terrine out of the mould, or you could serve the terrine directly from the mould. Choose fairly thick yogurt for preference.

Aubergine and courgette carpaccio with mozzarella cheese

Preparation time:
30 min, 3 hours
before

Cooking time: 10 min

Serves 6

**3 mozzarella
cheeses, 125 g
(4 oz) each**

3 small aubergines

3 small courgettes

olive oil

**1 tablespoon
chopped basil**

**1 tablespoon
chopped parsley**

**2 garlic cloves,
peeled and chopped**

coarse salt, pepper

1. Cut the aubergines into long slices about 2.5 mm ($\frac{1}{8}$ inch) thick. Layer them in a sieve with a sprinkling of coarse salt between the layers and leave for 2 hours. Prepare the courgettes in the same way but leave for only 1 hour.

2. Pre-heat the grill. Dry the aubergine and courgette slices on kitchen paper, place on a grill pan and grill briefly, then quickly turn the slices over. Put them on a dish, drizzle a little olive oil over them, sprinkle with the chopped herbs and garlic and leave to marinate for 1 hour.

3. Cut the mozzarella cheese into pieces. Roll a strip of vegetable around each and secure with a cocktail stick.

TASTE BITE

EXCELLENT with sliced ham, toast and anchovy fillets marinated in olive oil.

TIP

OTHER VEGETABLES, such as red, yellow and green peppers, tomatoes and fennel all go well with mozzarella cheese. Those that are unsuitable for the wrapping technique can simply be topped with a circle of cheese.

Pine nut tart

Preparation time:
30 min

Cooking time: 35 min

Serves 6

For the pastry:

**250 g (8 oz) plain
flour**

1 tablespoon sugar

1 egg

salt

125 g (4 oz) butter

For the filling:

**2 tablespoons
raisins**

2 tablespoons rum

**100 g (3¹/₂ oz)
softened butter**

50 g (2 oz) sugar

2 eggs

**50 g (2 oz) ground
almonds**

**100 g (3¹/₂ oz) pine
nuts**

TASTE BITE

THIS TART is particularly
delicious with apricot
compote.

1. For the pastry: sift the flour into a mixing bowl, make a well in the centre and put the sugar, salt and egg into it.

2. Add the butter in small pieces and mix together rapidly by hand. Roll the pastry into a ball, wrap it in a floured cloth and leave for 2 hours in a cool place.

3. For the filling: put the raisins to soak in the rum, drain any rum that is not absorbed. Beat the butter and sugar together in a mixing bowl. In another bowl, beat the eggs together with the ground almonds. Gradually add the butter and sugar mixture, then the raisins, and 75 g (3 oz) of the pine nuts. Set aside.

4. Pre-heat the oven to 200°C (400°F), Gas Mark 6. Lightly flour the work surface and roll out the pastry. Line a flan tin with it and crimp the border. Fill with the pine nut mixture and sprinkle the remaining nuts on the top. Bake for 35 minutes, or until the top is firm and golden brown.

Corsican cheesecake (Fiadone)

Preparation time:
20 min

Cooking time: 1 hour

Serves 6

750 g (1½ lb) ricotta cheese

5 eggs, separated

175 g (6 oz) sugar

grated rind of 1 lemon

groundnut oil

salt

1. Pre-heat the oven to 160°C (325°F), Gas Mark 3. Grease and flour a 23-cm (9-inch) springform cake tin.

2. Cream the ricotta until smooth in a food processor, or by rubbing through a sieve. Whisk the egg yolks with the sugar in a mixing bowl until white and creamy.

3. Add the ricotta gradually to the egg and sugar batter, together with the lemon rind. Add a pinch of salt to the egg whites and whisk until stiff then fold gently into the mixture. Make sure the mixture is fully blended but take care not to over-mix.

4. Pour into the cake tin and smooth the top with a wet spatula. Bake for about 1 hour, or until the top is golden brown and the cheesecake pulls away from the sides of the tin. Turn out on to a wire rack to cool.

TASTE BITE

EXCELLENT eaten warm the same day or cold the following day, with a fruit salad or a fruit compote made with apricots, peaches and almonds, accompanied by a dessert wine.

Fresh goat's cheese with figs

Preparation time:
25 min, 2 hours
in advance

Needs no cooking

Serves 6

**400 g (13 oz) fresh
goat's cheese**

**75 g (3 oz) whole
blanched almonds**

**400 g (13 oz) purple
figs**

6 basil sprigs

salt, pepper

1. Pre-heat the oven to 180°C (350°F)
Gas Mark 4. Roughly chop the basil
leaves. Smooth the goat's cheese in a
food processor or push through a sieve.
Season with salt and pepper and add
the basil.

2. Roughly chop the almonds, toast in
the oven until golden brown and set
aside. Watch carefully as the almonds
can burn easily. Remove the stalks from
the figs.

3. Roll the figs by hand in the cheese
until they are completely coated then
press in the chopped almonds all over
the cheese surface. Leave for 2 hours
in a cool place.

4. Cut each fig in half to display the
fruit in the centre.

TIP

THE SAME CHEESE MIX-
TURE can be used to coat
large grapes. Pistachio nuts
may be used in place of the
almonds. Choose cheeses
that are not too wet or the
preparation will be too sticky
to handle easily.

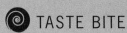 TASTE BITE

VERY GOOD with walnut
bread, wholegrain bread or
poppy seed rolls, accom-
panied by a fruity white
wine.

beneath
the pines

Pimiento boats with lightly-salted cod filling

Preparation time:
35 min, 2 hours in
advance

Cooking time: 20 min

Serves 6

375 g (12 oz) cod fillet

18 mild green pimientos or 9 green peppers, halved

2 salad potatoes, peeled

1 garlic clove, peeled

7 tablespoons crème fraîche

1 tablespoon chopped chives

curry powder

olive oil

sea salt

salt, pepper

1. Sprinkle sea salt liberally on the cod and leave in a cool place.

2. Hold the pimientos in a gas flame or put under a hot grill for 2 minutes to blister the skin. Put in a plastic bag for 10 minutes before skinning.

3. Slit the pimientos lengthways and remove the pith and seeds. Cook the potatoes in boiling salted water for 20 minutes or until soft.

4. Wash the cod under running water, pat dry with kitchen paper and place in a saucepan of water. Bring up to a gentle simmer then turn off the heat and leave the fish to poach in the hot water for 5 minutes.

5. Blend the fish with the garlic in a food processor. Mash the potatoes and mix with the fish, then add the crème fraîche and enough olive oil to make the mixture creamy. Stir in the chives.

6. Fill the halves of pimiento with this mixture and lightly dust with curry powder.

TASTE BITE

SERVE WITH CROUTONS rubbed with garlic and olive oil.

TIP

THESE DELICATE PIMIEN-TOS, in season around mid-August, are quickly past their best and need preparing as soon as possible after they are bought. The recipe can also be made with red peppers.

Tuna à la tartare with mustard seed

Preparation time: 20 min

Marinade: 1 hour

Needs no cooking

Serves 6

625 g ('/₄ lb) fresh tuna fillet

2 teaspoons hot-flavoured mustard

3 tablespoons olive oil

'/₄ teaspoon grated lemon rind

1 bunch of chives, coarsely chopped

1 bunch of dill, coarsely chopped

2 teaspoons mustard seed

'/₂ teaspoon fine salt

1 teaspoon coarsely ground coriander seeds

lemon juice

sea salt, pepper

1. Lay the tuna flat on a board and cut into thin strips then into cubes.

2. In a basin, mix the hot mustard with the olive oil. Add the cubed tuna, grated lemon rind and 4 tablespoons chopped herbs. Season with pepper and mix well, then add the mustard seed, the fine salt and the coriander seeds. Stir thoroughly.

3. Set aside in a cool place for 1 hour. Sprinkle with lemon juice before serving.

Cold patties with gazpacho sauce

Preparation time:
40 min

Cooking time: 30 min

Serves 6

For the patties:

1 thick slice ham
with its fat, or
Parma ham

200 g (7 oz)
sausagemeat

¹/₂ onion

3 garlic cloves

1 bunch of parsley

3-4 eggs

5 handfuls stale
white bread, made
into crumbs

3 tablespoons
groundnut oil

500 g (1 lb)
passata (crushed
tomatoes)

sea salt, pepper

**For the gazpacho
sauce:**

750 g (1¹/₂ lb)
tomatoes

2 onions

1 cucumber

2 red peppers

1 garlic clove

1 tablespoon wine
vinegar

2 tablespoons olive
oil

1 green pepper

salt, pepper

1. For the patties: Remove the rind from the ham, coarsely chop and mix into the sausagemeat. Finely chop the onion, garlic and parsley.

2. Combine the meats with 3 eggs, the chopped onion, garlic, parsley and the breadcrumbs, season with salt and pepper and mix well. The resulting mixture should be quite soft. Add another egg yolk if necessary.

3. Heat the groundnut oil in a frying pan and drop in spoonfuls of the mixture, flattening them to form round patties. Brown the patties on both sides and drain on kitchen paper.

4. Heat the passata in a pan, add the patties and cook for 30 minutes over low heat. Remove the patties and drain. Transfer the passata sauce to a food processor.

5. For the gazpacho sauce: skin and deseed the tomatoes, chop the flesh. Coarsely chop the onions, a quarter of the cucumber and 1 deseeded red pepper. Crush the garlic. Add all these ingredients to the passata sauce in the food processor together with the wine vinegar and olive oil. Blend to a creamy consistency, season, and refrigerate for 3 hours.

6. Prepare the rest of the vegetables into crudités and serve them with the patties and the gazpacho sauce.

TASTE BITE

THE PATTIES will be all the better if prepared the day before. The gazpacho, with ice cubes added to chill and dilute it, can also be served as a soup. Pack it in an insulated container.

Squid stuffed with herbs

Preparation time:
45 min

Cooking time:
35–40 mins

Serves 6

6 squid

1 shallot

1 garlic clove

1 small bunch each of: chives, basil, parsley

6 slices rough country bread

1 egg

2 tablespoons brandy

350 g (12 oz) passata (crushed tomatoes)

1 bunch of thyme

2 bay leaves

olive oil

1. Detach the heads and tentacles of the squid from the body pouch. Remove the intestines, eyes and the hard 'beak' from the centre of the tentacles. Clean out the pouches, taking care not to split them. Peel off the thin purple covering membrane, rinse well and leave to drain.

2. Peel and chop the shallot and garlic. Coarsely chop the herbs. Cut the crusts from the bread, lightly toast the slices and make into breadcrumbs.

3. Soften the shallot gently in 1 tablespoon of olive oil. Add the tentacles, roughly chopped and, as soon as they have stiffened and turned white, remove from the heat and stir in the breadcrumbs, garlic and herbs. Add the egg and mix to a paste.

4. Preheat the oven to 180°C (350°F), Gas Mark 4. Fill the squid pouches with the mixture and pin the opening securely with a cocktail stick. Season the passata with salt and pepper if necessary and add the brandy, thyme bay leaves. Put into an ovenproof dish and lay the squid in it.

5. Cook for 35 to 40 minutes, turning the squid half way through. Set aside to get cold.

 TASTE BITE

EXCELLENT WITH SLICES OF BREAD impregnated with tomato and sprinkled with olive oil (see Step 3 in recipe, page 62)

TIP

DO NOT OVERFILL the squid pouches or they may burst during cooking. Turn them over with a spatula rather than a fork, which could puncture them.

Mussels in a marinade

Preparation time:
25 min

Refrigeration:
3 hours

Cooking time:
10–15 min

Serves 6

TIP

YOU COULD TRANSPORT the mussels still in their shells, if preferred.

1 kg (2 lb) large mussels

3¹/₂ tablespoons dry white wine

4 tablespoons lemon juice

1 bay leaf

1 garlic clove, peeled and chopped

1 red onion, peeled

¹/₂ lemon

1 bunch of chives

4 mint sprigs

1 tablespoon pink peppercorns

salt, pepper

1. Scrape the mussel shells clean, remove the beards and wash under running water. Put them in a large pan, cover and cook over low heat until they open, discarding any that remain shut. Take the mussels out of the shells and set aside in a terrine.

2. Drain off the cooking liquor (about 200 ml/7 fl oz) through a sieve lined with muslin into a saucepan.

3. Add the wine, lemon juice, bay leaf and garlic to the mussel liquor, season with salt and pepper and simmer for 5 minutes.

4. Slice the onion into rings. Finely slice the half lemon. Put the onion rings and lemon slices into the terrine with the mussels.

5. Chop the chives and add to the terrrine with the mint leaves and the peppercorns. Pour on the boiled marinade, stir well and allow to cool. Refrigerate for 3 hours.

TASTE BITE

VERY GOOD with slices of bread spread with lightly salted butter, or spiced butter (see recipe for red butter, page 36). Or with bread impregnated with tomato (see Step 3 in recipe, page 62).

Gambas (jumbo prawns) marinated in peppered oil

Preparation time:
20 min

Cooking time: 10 min

Marinade: 3 hours

Serves 6

12 very large jumbo prawns

1 bouquet garni

white vinegar

3 red peppers

2 yellow peppers

1 teaspoon cayenne pepper (or Espelette pepper if available)

4 tablespoons olive oil

coarse cooking salt

1. Boil 1.5 litres (2½ pints) water with a handful of coarse salt and the bouquet garni. Add 7 tablespoons of white vinegar and leave to cook for 5 minutes then drop in the prawns and cook for 2 to 4 minutes, according to the size. Drain and refresh them immediately in cold water.

2. Remove the pith and seeds from the peppers and cut into strips. Add 1 tablespoon of coarse salt and a touch of white vinegar to ½ litre (17 fl oz) water and bring to the boil. Cook the peppers for 2 minutes in this, then drain and refresh in cold water.

3. Mix 1 teaspoon of cayenne pepper with the olive oil and pour over the prawns and peppers. Leave in a cool place for 3 hours.

TIP

IF FRESH JUMBO PRAWNS are unavailable use frozen ones, following the defrosting instructions carefully before cooking in Step 1.

Three kinds of tortilla (Spanish omelette): piperade, herbs, cheese

Preparation time:
30 min

Cooking time: 1 hour

Serves 6

piperade tortilla:

8 eggs

250 g (8 oz) each peppers and onions

2 garlic cloves

1 slice ham, cut from the bone

1 bouquet garni

500 g (1 lb) tomatoes

2 teaspoons sugar

olive oil

salt, pepper

herb tortilla:

6 eggs

1 bunch of parsley

1/2 bunch of chives

2 tarragon sprigs

2 garlic cloves

olive oil

salt, pepper

cheese tortilla:

6 eggs

150 g (5 oz) grated pecorino cheese (or other hard, strong cheese)

200 ml (7 fl oz) milk

1 garlic clove

cayenne pepper

olive oil

salt, pepper

1. For the piperade, remove the stems and seeds from the peppers and cut the flesh into pieces. Peel and chop the onions. Peel and chop the garlic.

2. Cut off the rind and fat from the ham and put in a non-stick frying pan to render the fat. Add the onions, the ham, cut in cubes, garlic and peppers.

3. Mix thoroughly, add the bouquet garni and leave to cook gently for 15 minutes then add the tomatoes, skinned, deseeded and chopped. Season with salt and pepper and add the sugar. Cook over fairly brisk heat until all the water has evaporated. Leave to cool then remove the bouquet garni and ham rind.

4. Beat the eggs, season with salt and pepper then mix in the piperade. Heat a little olive oil in an omelette pan and pour in the mixture. When the eggs begin to set, turn the tortilla over and finish cooking on the other side.

5. Make the other two tortillas in the same way, one with the chopped herbs and chopped garlic, the other with the grated pecorino, chopped garlic and 2 pinches of cayenne pepper. For the cheese tortilla, beat the eggs with the milk.

6. Stack the tortillas in layers. When cold, cut into portions and spike each with a cocktail stick to keep the layers together. Pack in an airtight container.

TASTE BITE

EXCELLENT served on large slices of bread. It is also good with potatoes. It is the classic Spanish tortilla – thick and high in fat, but so delicious.

TIP

DON'T STIR THE EGGS during cooking as this will make the omelettes more difficult to cut.

Tapas: ham with figs; pancetta with melon; smoked duck breast with apricots

Preparation time:
20 min, 2 hours
before

Needs no cooking

6 slices ham (use a lean, good-quality ham)

12 slices round pancetta

100 gm (3¹/₂ oz) smoked duck breast

6 figs

6 apricots

1 melon

1. Cut the figs and apricots into quarters. Halve the melon and remove the seeds, then cut into quarters.

2. Remove the melon rind and cut the flesh into pieces. Put all the fruit in the refrigerator for 2 hours.

3. Remove the fat from the duck breast and the rind from the ham. With cocktail sticks, affix pieces of duck breast to the apricot quarters, the pancetta to the melon and pieces of the ham, folded, to the figs.

-ⓦ- TIP
EACH LITTLE TAPAS can be placed on a slice of crusty baguette.

Tartlets with ricotta and cheese filling

Preparation time:
20 min

Refrigeration:
2 hours

Cooking time: 25 min

Serves 6

For the pastry:

150 g (5 oz) plain flour

1 vanilla pod

125 g (4 oz) butter

salt

For the filling:

100 g (3¹/₂ oz) Manchego cheese (or a good medium-hard cheese)

60 g (2¹/₂ oz) butter

250 g (8 oz) ricotta cheese

4 eggs, separated

150 g (5 oz) sugar

2 tablespoons cornflour

100 ml (3¹/₂ oz) crème fraîche

grated rind of 1 lemon

1. To make the pastry, put the flour with a pinch of salt into a mixing bowl. Split the vanilla pod, scrape out the black seeds and add to the flour.

2. Cut the butter into cubes and rub in lightly. Add 2–3 tablespoons water gradually and bind together to a dough. Form into a ball and leave covered in the refrigerator for 2 hours.

3. Preheat the oven to 180°C (350°F), Gas Mark 4). Roll out the pastry on a floured work surface and line 6 tartlet tins.

4. For the filling, shave the Manchego cheese into thin slivers with a potato peeler. Melt the butter over low heat.

5. Whisk the egg yolks with the sugar until white and frothy, add the potato starch, ricotta, crème fraîche, butter and lemon rind.

6. Whip the egg whites to stiff peaks and gently fold in. Fill the tartlet cases and scatter with half the Manchego slivers. Bake for 25 minutes. Scatter the remaining Manchego over the tartlets as soon as they come from the oven.

country
parks

Cottage cheese with herbs and white wine on crusty bread

Preparation time:
15 min

Draining time:
1 hour

No cooking needed

Serves 6

500 g (1 lb) cottage cheese

2 spring onions

1 white shallot

¹/₂ bunch each of: flat-leaf parsley, chives, chervil

1 thyme sprig

3 tablespoons white wine

1 teaspoon sherry vinegar

1 teaspoon olive oil

125 g (4 oz) mascarpone

salt, pepper

1. Put the cottage cheese into a strainer and allow to drain for 1 hour. Peel and chop the spring onions and shallot. Chop the herbs briefly in a processor or herb mill.

2. Crush the cheese with a fork then beat it with a spatula until it is smooth. Add the spring onions, shallot and herbs and season with salt and pepper.

3. Stir in the white wine, sherry vinegar and a touch of olive oil. Leave in a cool place for 2 hours.

4. Whip the mascarpone and stir into the flavoured cottage cheese. Serve it on slices of fresh baguette.

TASTE BITE

PREPARE THE CHEESE the day before, so that the flavours have the chance to develop, but do not add the mascarpone until you are ready to prepare the picnic.

Duck terrine

Preparation time:
45 min
1 or 2 days before

Cooking time:
1¹/₂ hours

Serves 6

1 oven-ready duck

**150 g (5 oz) belly
of pork**

**300 g (10 oz) lean
pork**

**1 Russet or other
eating apple**

6 prunes

**3 tablespoons
brandy or Calvados**

**1 teaspoon mixed
freshly ground
pepper**

**1 or more duck
breasts, weighing
in total 450 g
(14 oz)**

coarse salt

fine salt

1. Pre-heat the oven to 180°C (350°F), Gas Mark 4. Skin the duck and cut off the breast meat. Remove the legs and bone them. Cut the breast and leg meat, which should weigh about 300 g (10 oz), into small cubes.

2. Roughly cut up the 2 kinds of pork meat and grind it in the food processor, using the pulse control so as not to overheat the mixture. Peel the apple and chop it finely. Stone the prunes and cut into pieces.

3. Add the apple, duck meat, brandy, 2 good pinches of coarse salt and mixed ground pepper to the pork mixture.

4. Skin the duck breast and cut it into strips. Season with salt.

5. Spread a layer of the prepared mixture in the bottom of a terrine and press well down. Cover with strips of duck breast and a few pieces of prune. Continue to layer the rest of the ingredients in the same way.

6. Put the terrrine, uncovered, in a roasting tin filled with hot water to halfway and cook for 1¹/₂ hours. Remove the terrine and set aside to cool. When still just tepid, cover with foil-wrapped card and place a weight on top. Refrigerate until the next day. Keep in the terrine to take to the picnic.

TASTE BITE
EXCELLENT on slices of rough country bread, with a few leaves of rocket or dandelion and pickled gherkins.

TIP
THE PRUNES could be replaced by mushrooms. Always include a good proportion of fat in the ingredients.

Chicken and aubergine flan

Preparation time:
45 min the previous
day or 2 hours
in advance

Cooking time: 35 min

Serves 6

For the pastry:

**175 g (6 oz) plain
flour**

**100 g (3¹/₂ oz)
butter**

1 pinch salt

For the filling:

**3 large chicken
breasts, skinned
and boned**

**1 jar aubergines
conserved in oil**

3 thyme sprigs

3 bay leaves

**100 g (3¹/₂ oz)
tapenade
(see page 125)**

olive oil

salt

 TIP

IF SHORT OF TIME, use 250 g
(8 oz) of ready-made shortcrust pastry.

1. For the pastry, put the flour with a pinch of salt in a mixing bowl. Cut the butter into small dice and lightly rub into the flour.

2. Gradually add 1-2 tablespoons water to bind into a dough, handling the pastry as little as possible. Form into a ball and refrigerate.

3. Pre-heat the oven to 200°C (400°F), Gas Mark 6.

4. Oil 3 rectangles of kitchen foil and place one breast on each. Season with salt and pepper and top with a sprig of thyme and a bay leaf. Drizzle with olive oil.

5. Fold the foil over and seal the edges to make 3 packages. Place on a baking tray and bake for 15 minutes. Check that the breasts are cooked through by inserting a thin, sharp skewer.

6. Grease and flour a 20-cm (8-inch) flan tin. Roll out the pastry on a lightly floured surface and line the tin, pressing the pastry to exclude trapped air, then prick the base all over with a fork. Bake for 15 to 20 minutes. Remove from the oven and when cool spread the tapenade over the base.

7. Drain the aubergines on kitchen paper. Remove the chicken breasts from the foil and cut into slices. Fill the pastry case, alternating slices of meat with the aubergines.

Mushroom parcels

Preparation time:
20 min

Cooking time: 30 min

Serves 6

**24 large button
mushrooms**

$\frac{1}{2}$ lemon

3 slices bread

**1 bunch of flat-leaf
parsley**

3 basil sprigs

**200 g (7 oz) boiled
ham**

**3 tablespoons
crème fraîche**

1 egg, beaten

**3$\frac{1}{2}$ tablespoons
Madeira or Muscat
(or any dessert
wine)**

1 bunch of chives

olive oil

salt, pepper

1. Pre-heat the oven to 180°C (350°F), Gas Mark 4. Remove the mushroom stalks and slightly enlarge the cavity in the cups to accommodate the stuffing. Rub them over with the cut side of the lemon.

2. For the stuffing: lightly toast the bread and crush into breadcrumbs. Chop the basil and parsley.

3. Remove any rind from the ham and chop it in a food processor. Mix the breadcrumbs with the egg, ham, 4 tablespoons of chopped herbs, the crème fraîche and the Madeira. Season with salt and pepper.

4. Oil all the mushroom caps and season them with salt and pepper.

5. Fill 12 of the mushroom caps with the stuffing and cover with the remaining 12. Place on a baking sheet and bake for 25 to 30 minutes, until they are browned and the stuffing is firm. Leave to cool.

 TASTE BITE

EAT THE PARCELS COLD with a few drops of ketchup or Tabasco.

TIP

TO MAKE THE PARCELS EASIER to transport and pretty to look at, blanch some long chive leaves for 2 seconds in boiling water to soften them and use them to tie up the mushroom parcels.

Wild mushroom turnovers

Preparation time:
25 min

Cooking time: 50 min

Serves 6
(2 turnovers)

**750 g (1½ lb) mixed
wild mushrooms, or
mixed commercial
mushrooms
(shiitake, oyster,
chestnut...)**

**2 small leeks (white
part with some
green)**

25 g (1 oz) butter

**1 tablespoon rice
flour**

**4 tablespoons
crème fraîche**

1 tablespoon port

**2 circles puff
pastry**

1 egg, beaten

salt, pepper

1. Pre-heat the oven to 200°C (400°F), Gas Mark 5). Cut the mushrooms into pieces, salt them and sweat them in a covered sauté pan, over moderate heat, for 5 minutes. Drain and reserve the liquor.

2. Cut the leeks into rings. Heat the butter in a sauté pan and cook the leeks gently over low heat for 10 minutes. Add the mushrooms, season with pepper and cook for 5 minutes or until they have browned.

3. Mix the rice flour into the liquor sweated from the mushrooms, add the crème fraîche and the port and cook for 1 minute to thicken. Lightly coat the leeks and mushrooms with this to give a good texture to the filling.

4. Lay the circles of pastry on the work surface and spread the filling over one half of each. Fold the other half of the pastry over to form a semi-circle, seal and crimp the edges. Brush the top with beaten egg to give a golden glaze. Place on a baking sheet and bake for 25 minutes.

TASTE BITE

GOOD HOT OR COLD. These are equally delicious made with ceps, which need no preliminary sweating. Simply slice them and lightly fry for 15 minutes. The addition of rice flour to the crème fraîche is also unnecessary, as the ceps contain a natural thickening agent.

TIP

IF YOU WANT to keep these turnovers hot, wrap them first in kitchen foil and then several layers of newspaper, which is an excellent insulator.

Harvester's terrine

Preparation time:
30 min, 2 days
before

Cooking time:
2³/₄ hours

Serves 6

500 g (1 lb) lean
pork belly, cut
into slices

750 g (1¹/₂ lb) shin
beef

2 bay leaves

2 peeled garlic
cloves

¹/₄ teaspoon Sichuan
pepper (or ground
mixed peppercorns)

1 bottle red Côtes-
du-Rhône

2 onions, peeled

2 carrots, peeled

2 cloves

1 bouquet garni

6 g (3 leaves)
gelatine

2 tablespoons
chopped parsley

olive oil

salt, black pepper

For the sauce:

1 candied orange
rind

3 pickled gherkins

250 g (8 oz)
mayonnaise

1 tablespoon
chopped parsley

TASTE BITE

POLENTA PANCAKES make
a pleasant change from
bread to eat with this dish.

1. Two days prior to serving, put the meat into a bowl, add the bay leaves, garlic and Sichuan pepper. Pour on enough wine to cover the meat. Cover the bowl and leave to marinate in the refrigerator until the following day.

2. Pre-heat the oven to 180°C (350°F), Gas Mark 4. Drain the meats, reserving the marinade with the bay leaves and garlic. Slice the onions in half and cut the carrots into chunks.

3. Brown the meat for 10 minutes in olive oil, season with salt and pepper and transfer to an oven-proof dish. In the same oil, brown the carrots and onions for 5 minutes then add to the meat.

4. Add the marinade, cloves, bouquet garni and remaining wine. Season with salt. Cover tightly with foil and cook for 2¹/₂ hours, or until ready. Check regularly.

5. Take out the meats and strain the cooking liquor through a sieve into a bowl. Soak the gelatine in cold water until soft, then squeeze it dry and add to the hot liquor. Stir until dissolved.

6. Cut the meats into cubes and mix with 2 tablespoons of chopped parsley. Place the meat in a terrine, pour the liquor over it and refrigerate until the next day.

7. For the sauce: finely chop the orange peel and gherkins and mix into the mayonnaise with the parsley.

Fruit and vanilla tart

Preparation time:
25 min, 3 hours
in advance

Cooking time: 25 min

Serves 6

**For the sweet
shortcrust pastry:**

**250 g (8 oz) plain
flour**

**75 g (3 oz) icing
sugar**

**150 g (5 oz)
softened butter**

1 egg

2 pinches salt

For the filling:

**500 g (1 lb) fruit,
e.g. blueberries,
blackcurrants,
plums, etc.**

**60 g (2¹/₂ oz) sugar,
or more according to
sweetness of fruit**

¹/₂ vanilla pod

**60 sponge finger
(Boudoir) biscuits**

icing sugar

1. To make the pastry, place the flour in a large bowl and add the salt. Sprinkle with the sugar then rub in the butter with the fingertips until the mixture resembles coarse breadcrumbs. Make a hollow in the centre, break the egg into it and begin mixing, still with the fingers, bringing the flour from the sides to the centre. Quickly form the mixture into a ball and put it to relax for 3 hours in a cool place.

2. Pre-heat the oven to 200°C (400°F), Gas Mark 6. Roll out the pastry on a floured surface and line a pie tin.

3. Rinse and prepare selected fruit. Drain on kitchen paper and put in a bowl with the sugar. Mix well. Slit the vanilla pod, scrape out the seeds and mix them with the fruit.

4. Crush the sponge finger biscuits by hand and scatter on the base of the pastry. Arrange the fruit on top and bake for 25 minutes. While the tart is still just warm, dredge it with icing sugar.

Autumn fruit salad

Preparation time:
25 min

Refrigeration:
2 hours

Cooking time: 10 min

Serves 6

1 lemon

50 g (2oz) sugar

1 bottle sweet Gaillac wine (or any other dessert wine)

2 star anise

6 dried apricots

6 pitted prunes

3 apples

3 pears

1 large bunch of Italian dessert grapes

50 g (2 oz) walnut halves

1. Take a thin strip of rind from the lemon. Pour the wine into a pan with the sugar and bring to the boil then add the lemon rind and star anise.

2. Cook gently for 5 minutes then remove from the heat. Add the apricots and prunes and leave them to soak while the liquid cools. Put into a serving bowl.

3. Peel and slice the apples and pears; halve and deseed the grapes, sprinkle with the juice from the lemon and add to the apricots and prunes. Add the walnuts and stir together everything in the serving bowl. Refrigerate for 2 hours.

TASTE BITE

ADD A LITTLE CHOPPED MINT just before serving this dessert at your picnic, and remember to take along some sponge finger biscuits to eat with it.

 TIP

THE INGREDIENTS of this easy-to-prepare fruit salad can be varied with the seasons: cherries and strawberries in the spring, peaches and apricots in summer.

a pause
on the
ski
slopes

Tabbouleh with dried fruit

Preparation time:
40 min

Cooking time: 10 min

Serves 6

**300 g (10 oz)
coarse-grain
couscous**

1 bunch of mint

**1 large bunch of
flat-leaf parsley**

6 dried apricots

**2 tablespoons
shelled walnuts**

**60 g (2¹/₂ oz)
raisins**

nutmeg

**8 tablespoons
lemon juice**

**4 tablespoons olive
oil**

salt, pepper

1. Cook the couscous according to the maker's instructions on the pack.

2. Chop the mint and the parsley. Cut the apricots into small pieces and coarsely chop the walnuts.

3. When the couscous is cooked, leave it to rest for 10 minutes in a bowl before stirring it and checking there are no lumps. Add the apricots, raisins, walnuts and herbs. Mix well and season with pepper and a good pinch of nutmeg.

4. Mix the lemon juice and olive oil together thoroughly and stir into the tabbouleh.

TASTE BITE

IT IS THE QUALITY of the herbs that gives this dish its fresh flavour. A few pistachio nuts may also be added.

TIP

IF IT CAN BE FOUND in specialist shops, quinoa, known as Inca rice, is the best grain for this recipe. It is a South American cereal, similar to coarse, greyish-brown couscous. It has a higher protein content than wheat (15%) and is used in sweet and savoury dishes.

Ham, apple and raisin strudel

Preparation time:
25 min

Cooking time: 30 min

Serves 4
(2 strudels)

3 Bramley or Russet apples

50 g (2 oz) lightly salted butter

8 sheets filo pastry

4 thin slices ham (Aosta or Parma is good)

1–2 tablespoons sugar

2 tablespoons raisins

50 g (2 oz) walnut halves

icing sugar

ground cinnamon

TASTE BITE

EAT THE STRUDELS HOT OR JUST WARM. To keep them hot, store them in a tin wrapped in newspaper, inside an insulated bag.

TIP

STRUDEL is a sweet pastry of Austrian origin. In this savoury version the salt and sugar make a very successful combination.

1. Peel and slice the apples and put in a saucepan with half of the butter, the sugar and enough water just to cover the bottom of the pan. Cook gently for about 10 minutes until the apples are soft but not reduced to a purée. Remove from the heat and leave to cool.

2. Pre-heat the oven to 180°C (350°F), Gas Mark 4).

3. Melt the remaining butter. Lay 1 sheet of filo pastry on the work surface and brush it with the melted butter. Lay a second on top of the first, butter it and then add a third. The triple thickness gives the pastry body.

4. Lay 2 slices of ham on the pastry and spread with half the apple. Scatter half the raisins and nuts over the apple, leaving a 2.5-cm (1-inch) border of pastry all round. Prepare the second strudel with 3 of the remaining sheets of filo and the rest of the ingredients.

5. Carefully roll each strudel into a log shape. Dampen the edges and lay them on a baking sheet. Butter the last 2 sheets of filo, crumple them and lay them on top of the strudels to give volume. Sprinkle with cinnamon and icing sugar and bake for 20 minutes.

Pick-me-up soup

Preparation time:
25 min

Cooking time: 35 min

Serves 6

3 potatoes

2 shallots

2 celery sticks

3 carrots

1 tablespoon fresh ginger, chopped

300 g (10 oz) pearl barley, rinsed

1 thyme sprig

2 leeks

$\frac{1}{2}$ bunch of chervil, chopped

olive oil

salt, pepper

1. Cut the potatoes into cubes and chop the shallots. Slice the celery and shave the carrot into strips with a potato peeler.

2. Heat 2 tablespoons of olive oil in a saucepan.

3. Gently fry the shallots, add the potatoes and ginger, season with salt and pepper. Stir well and, without waiting for these ingredients to brown, gradually add 1.75 litres (3 pints) of water. Bring to the boil and add the pearl barley, thyme and celery. Cover, lower the heat and leave to cook for 15 minutes.

4. Add the leeks and carrot to the soup. Continue cooking for 10 more minutes then adjust the seasoning and stir in a few drops of olive oil. Chop the chervil leaves and stir into the soup.

5. Remove the thyme and pour the soup into an insulated container where it will keep hot until needed.

 TASTE BITE

FOR SIMPLICITY, the carrots may be diced and cooked together with the potatoes. Only the leeks then need to be added later.

TIP

BARLEY IS RICH IN calcium, phosphorus and potassium. For ease of cooking the husked grains are passed between 2 millstones. The resulting 'pearl' barley is prepared in the same way as rice.

Blue cheese and pear tartlets

Preparation time:
20 min

Cooking time: 8 min

Serves 6

1 pack puff pastry

3 pears (juicy, slightly acidic varieties)

300 g (10 oz) soft blue-veined cheese

2 tablespoons lemon juice

1 tablespoon crème fraîche

butter

1. Preheat the oven to 220°C (425°F), Gas Mark 7. Roll out the pastry, cut into circles and line 6 tartlet tins, leaving a little overhang as the pastry will shrink slightly while cooking. Set aside in the refrigerator.

2. Peel, core and thinly slice the pears. Sprinkle the slices with lemon juice to prevent discolouration.

3. Mash the cheese with a fork and mix with the crème fraîche. Divide this between the tartlets and arrange the strips of pear on the top. Bake for 7 to 8 minutes.

 TIP

TO ARRIVE INTACT, these tartlets need to travel in their tins so, for preference, use light-weight aluminium foil cases, from which the tartlets slip easily – ready to serve.

Cortina d'Ampezzo open sandwiches

Preparation time:
20 minutes,
1 hour in advance

Need no cooking

Serves 6

For the nut butter:

50 g (2 oz) butter

50 g (2 oz) walnut halves

For the sandwiches:

18 slices various salami and ham

100 g (3½ oz) young spinach leaves

50 g (2 oz) rocket

200 g (7 oz) Parmesan cheese

100 g (3½ oz) ricotta

2 sliced loaves

pepper

1. To make the walnut butter: finely grind the walnuts in a food processor and mix with the softened butter. Leave to set it in a cool place for 1 hour.

2. Remove the rinds from the meats. Strip the stems from the spinach leaves and rocket. Shave thin slices from the Parmesan with a potato peeler.

3. Blend the ricotta with a fork and spread on half of the bread slices. Spread the remaining slices with the walnut butter.

4. Place the Parmesan shavings and the rocket leaves on one half of the slices spread with ricotta and the spinach and boiled ham on the other half.

5. Top the slices spread with walnut butter with the remaining meats and a few spinach or rocket leaves.

TIP

WALNUT BUTTER HAS a delicious flavour when spread on sliced bread. Use it for sandwiches made with Cheddar and similar hard cheeses, as well as Gorgonzola, Dolcelatte, Bresse Bleu, together with a few fresh salad leaves. Hazelnuts or cashews can also be used to flavour butter.

Biscuit treats

Preparation time:
10 min

Cooking time:
6–7 min

Serves 4

For the biscuits:

100 g (3¹/₂ oz) butter

150 g (5 oz) plain flour

2 egg yolks

60 g (2¹/₂ oz) sugar

1 teaspoon baking powder

2 teaspoons grated fresh ginger

icing sugar

For the filling:

1 tin sweetened chestnut purée

60 g (2¹/₂ oz) shelled hazelnuts

◎ TASTE BITE

TOP THE BISCUIT SAND-WICHES with a cloud of whipped cream (an aerosol pack weighs very little in your back-pack).

1. Preheat the oven to 180°C (350°F), Gas Mark 4.

To make the biscuits: soften the butter to room temperature. Put the flour in a mixing bowl and rub in the butter until the mixture resembles coarse breadcrumbs. Set aside.

2. In another bowl, whisk the egg yolks with the sugar until white and frothy then add the flour-and-butter crumbs, baking powder and ginger. Combine quickly by hand and form into a ball. Set aside in a cool place for 20 minutes.

3. On a surface powdered with icing sugar, roll out the pastry to a thickness of 5 mm (¹/₄ inch). Cut into triangles with a pastry cutter or a sharp knife.

4. Place the biscuits on a non-stick baking sheet and bake for 6–7 minutes until the edges are browned. Leave to cool on a wire rack.

5. For the filling: coarsely chop the walnuts. Just before serving, spread the chestnut purée on half the biscuits and sprinkle on the chopped nuts. Top with the remaining halves to make a sandwich.

Wine mulled with orange and cinnamon

Preparation time: 10 min

Cooking time: 5 min

Serves 6

1 bottle red wine

1 orange, unwaxed or well scrubbed

1 cinnamon stick

6 brown sugar lumps

2 cloves

6 peppercorns

1. Peel a long, thin strip of rind from the orange, taking care to avoid the pith. Break the cinnamon stick into several pieces.

2. Put the wine into a saucepan with all the flavourings and heat it up slowly. If you wish to retain the alcohol content do not allow it to boil, otherwise let it simmer gently for 10 minutes to diffuse the spicy aromas. Put it in a vacuum flask until required.

 TIP

USE A FULL-BODIED WINE, such as a Côtes-du-Rhone, Corbière or a Coteau-du-Languedoc.

TASTE BITE

EXCELLENT to drink with hot chestnuts or with Pine Nut Tart (see page 70) and Fruit and Vanilla Tart (see page 105).

Ten tips for a successful picnic

1. Don't forget to pack a tin-opener, a sharp knife and a corkscrew – or a Swiss army knife, which miraculously performs all these functions.

2. Remember to pack paper napkins, plenty of paper plates (as you need a layer of 2–3 per person to make a steady plate) and a roll of kitchen paper.

3. Take along some black rubbish sacks in the interests of keeping the countryside tidy.

4. Store all the prepared items in airtight containers, insulated jars or cool bags (especially in hot weather, when things dry out very quickly).

5. Wrap sandwiches in clingfilm or foil, to keep the fillings from escaping.

6. Pack tartlets and small prepared dishes in insulated bags, ice-boxes or baskets to make sure they do not rattle around.

7. Pack the most fragile ingredients on the top of less delicate items: putting a terrine on top of hard-boiled eggs and tomatoes is not a good idea!

8. Leave flans in the dishes they were cooked in. Aluminium foil dishes are ideal as they are light to carry and disposable.

9. Remember to take full water bottles. In hot weather you need at least a $\frac{1}{2}$ litre (1 pint) per person. And don't forget the disposable drinking cups. Plastic nets, too, are useful for cooling bottles of wine or water in the river but be sure to anchor them well or you may see your drinks floating away on the current!

10. A vacuum flask for tea, coffee or mulled wine is indispensable in winter time.

Basic recipes

PASTRY AND DOUGH

Shortcrust pastry
(p.98): the classic pastry for quiches and vegetable flans

Sweet shortcrust pastry
(p.70): ideal for all fruit tarts

Bread dough
(p.63): it is easy to make in a food processor but needs to be left to prove, or the result will be hard and brittle. It is the ideal base for pissaladière, pizza and certain open sandwiches. Supermarkets stock pizza bases and semi-baked bread rolls, just needing a final bake at home.

Shortbread dough
(p.105): an alternative classic recipe to use when making fruit tarts and crumbles.

TIP
BUTTERING THE BREAD helps to keep sandwiches moist. It also enhances the flavours. Mayonnaise, bought in tubes or jars is indeed easy to transport but home-made mayonnaise is so much nicer and can be flavoured in many ways: with garlic, herbs, condiments, spices, etc.

SAUCES

Red butter (p.36): for open sandwiches based on raw, smoked or cooked fish.

Walnut butter (p.117): a high-calorie spread that is perfect in sandwiches after a long autumn or winter hike. Especially good with cold meats.

Herb mayonnaise (p.34)

Tartare sauce (p.10): ideal with crudités, roasts and cold chicken.

Guacamole (p.10): the commercially available ones are often acid and contain too much garlic. Good guacamole is delicious with Mexican tacos or on pitta bread.

Cottage cheese with herbs (p.10): for open sandwiches and crudités.

Mint sauce (p.48): for use with all cold meats.

Tapenade (pp.67, 98): a thick paste made from capers, anchovies, olives, olive oil, lemon juice and seasoning. Commercial varieties in jars are widely available.

TIP
READY-MADE PASTRY, bought from the super-market, is very practical. There is no need to make puff pastry, unless you really like to, but other kinds only take a few minutes to pre-pare in a food processor or even by hand.

fishing trips and lakesides

moors and hills

punting along a river

beaches and sand dunes

beneath the pines

a pause on the ski slopes

country parks

This book first published by EPA, a division of
Hachette-Livre, 43 Quai de Grenelle,
Paris 75905, Cedex 15, France.

© 2001 EPA – Hachette-Livre, Paris
under the title Pique-Niques

Language translation produced by Translate-A-Book,
Oxford

Typesetting: Organ Graphic, Abingdon

© 2003 English translation, Octopus Publishing
Group Ltd, London

This edition published by Hachette Illustrated UK,
Octopus Publishing Group, 2–4 Heron Quays,
London E14 4JP

Editor
Joan Le Boru

Artistic design
Nancy Dorking

Layout
Nadine Gautier-Quentin

Platemaking: Eurésys, à Baisieux

Printing: Tien Wah Press

Registration of copyright: 09540 – June 2001

ISBN : 1844300110